SPICY HOT COLORS

SHERRY SHAHAN

Illustrated by PAULA BARRAGÁN

COLORES PICANTES

AUGUST HOUSE
LittleFolk

Published 2004 by August House LittleFolk.
P.O. Box 3223. Little Rock. Arkansas 72203
501-372-5450
http://www.augusthouse.com

Book design by Mina Greenstein
Manufactured in China
10   9   8   7   6   5   4   3   2   1   HC

LIBRARY OF CONGRESS CATALOGING-IN-PUBLICATION DATA
Shahan, Sherry.
Spicy hot colors: colores picantes / Sherry Shahan : illustrated by Paula Berragán.
p. cm.
English and Spanish.
ISBN 0-87483-741-3 (alk.paper)
1. Colors. 2. Colors—Psychological aspects. I. Barragán. Paula. 1963- II. Title.
QC495.8.S53 2004
535.6—dc22   2004040990

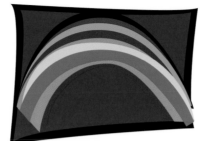

For my mother, Sylvia, and
two daughters,
Kristina Michelle and Kyle Shannon.
con amor
—SS

For Pablo—XO
—PB

Red as chili sauce
Drip-drop
Spicy hot

Red as firecrackers
Snap! Bang!
Bebop Pop!

RED   ROJO

Orange as sarapes
Sizzling lap wraps

Orange as roosters
Flitter-flutter
Flap!

ORANGE ANARANJADO

Yellow as gourds
    spitter-sputter seeds
Yellow as cobs of corn
    hip-hoppin' treat
YELLOW *AMARILLO*

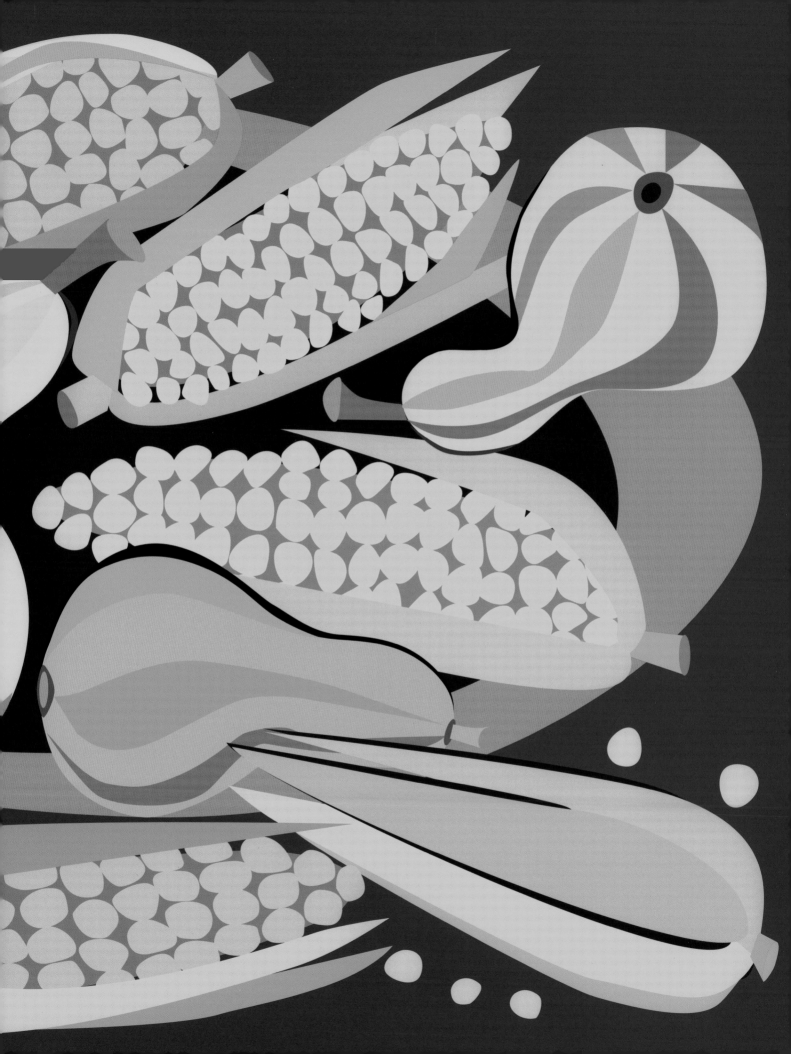

Green as Mexican iguanas
Slither
Slide
Samba!

Green as cilantro and cactus
Wiggle
Waggle
Rumba!

GREEN   VERDE

Purple as piñatas
Smack! Whack!
Spin on the ground

Purple as hard candy
Twist-Drop
Swivel around

PURPLE *MORADO*

Blue as tin angels
zinging on a string

Blue as paper dragons
Boogie-woogie
Swing!

BLUE AZUL

Brown as buñuelos
a crisp crunchy sound

Brown as a guitar
Pluck! Pluck!
Gettin' low down

BROWN   PARDO

Black as castanets
clickety-clickety
clack-clack

Black as boot heels
rat-a-tat
Flick-flack
BLACK NEGRO

White as sombreros
heel-toe hat dances

White as toy skeletons
rattle-rap
Razzmatazz!

WHITE

BLANCO

The spicy hot colors sizzle
on a Saturday night.
be-bop-bolero
bim-bam-la-bomba
La Cucaracha!
¡OLÉ!

VOCABULARY

Buñuelos Puffs of fried dough sprinkled with sugar and cinnamon.

Cactus A spiny plant that grows in hot, dry regions.

Castanets A pair of small shell-shaped instruments held in the hand. One shell is clicked against the other.

Cilantro The lacy leaves of this herb are used to flavor spicy dishes.

La Cucaracha A world-famous Mexican song about a cockroach.

Mexican hat dance A traditional heel-and-toe dance stepped around a *sombrero*.

Mexican iguana A large green lizard.

Paper dragons and tin angels
Playful decorations used in festivals.

Piñata A brightly colored papier-mâché container filled with candy, fruit, and toys. Children are blindfolded and given a stick to break the piñata, which is hung above their heads.

Sarape A colorful shawl or blanket.

Skeletons Used in a festival called Day of the Dead. Despite its name, it isn't a spooky time, like Halloween. Participants celebrate loved ones who are no longer living.

Sombrero A broad-brimmed hat worn in the southwestern United States, Mexico, and Spain.

PRONUNCIATION

Amarillo (ah-mah-REEL-yoh)

Anaranjado (ah-nah-rahn-HA-do)

Azul (ah-SOOL)

Blanco (BLAHN-koh)

Buñuelos (Boo-NYWAH-los)

La Cucaracha (la koo-ka-RA-cha)

Morado (mor-RAH-do)

Negro (NEH-groh)

Olé (o-LEH)

Pardo (PAHR-doh)

Piñata (pee-NYA-ta)

Rojo (ROH-hoh)

Sarape (ser-RAH-pay)

Sombreros (sohm-BREH-ros)

Verde (VEHR-deh)

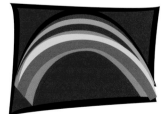